This book belongs to

MARTIN LEMAN'S

Little Kitten Book

A collection of pictures and rhymes

PELHAM BOOKS

*L*ady Queen Anne she sits in the sun,
As fair as a lily, as white as a swan;
Come taste my lily, come smell my rose,
Which of my maidens do you choose?
The ball is ours and none of yours,
Go to the wood and gather flowers.
Cats and kittens now stay within,
While we young maidens walk out and in.

Bubble and Squeak

$\mathcal{L}$ittle Blue Ben, who lives in the glen,
Keeps a blue cat and one blue hen,
Which lays of blue eggs a score and ten;
Where shall I find the little Blue Ben?

Dorabella

*H*igglety, piggglety, pop!
The dog has eaten the mop;
The pig's in a hurry,
The cat's in a flurry,
Higgglety, pigggletty, pop!

Snowball

*S*ix little mice sat down to spin;
Pussy passed by and she peeped in.
What are you doing, my little men?
Weaving coats for gentlemen.
Shall I come in and cut off your threads?
No, no, Mistress Pussy, you'd bite off our heads.
Oh, no, I'll not; I'll help you to spin.
That may be so, but you don't come in.

Jake

The rose is red, the grass is green,
Serve Queen Bess our noble queen.
   Kitty the spinner
   Will sit down to dinner,
And eat the leg of a frog:
   All you good people
   Look over the steeple,
And see the cat play with the dog.

Scruffty

Who's that ringing at my door bell?
A little pussy cat that isn't very well.
Rub its little nose with a little mutton fat,
That's the best cure for a little pussy cat.

Swee' pea

*L*ucy Locket lost her pocket
Kitty Fisher found it;
Not a penny was there in it,
Only ribbon round it.

First Christmas

Dame Trot and her cat
Sat down for a chat.
The Dame sat on this side
The cat sat on that.
Puss says the Dame
Can you catch a rat
Or a mouse in the dark?
Purr says the cat.

Weeny

Hey diddle, diddle,
The cat and the fiddle,
The cow jumped over the moon;
The little dog laughed
To see such sport,
And the dish ran away with the spoon.

Tiny Tom

Old Mother Shuttle
Lived in a coal-scuttle
Along with her dog and her cat;
What they ate I can't tell,
But 'tis known very well
That not one of the party was fat.
Old Mother Shuttle
Scoured out the coal-scuttle,
And washed both her dog and her cat;
The cat scratched her nose,
So they came to hard blows,
And who was the gainer by that?

Sooty

Ding, Dong, bell,
Pussy's in the well.
Who put her in?
Little Johnny Green.
Who pulled her out?
Little Tommy Stout.

What a naughty boy was that
To try to drown poor pussy cat,
Who never did any harm,
And killed the mice in his father's barn.

Russell

Bramble

PELHAM BOOKS/Stephen Greene Press

Published by the Penguin Group 27 Wrights Lane, London W8 5TZ, England
Viking Penguin Inc., 40 West 23rd Street, New York, New York 10010 USA
The Stephen Greene Press Inc., 15 Muzzey Street Lexington, Massachusetts 02173, USA
Penguin Books Australia Ltd, Registered, Victoria, Australia
Penguin Books Canada Ltd, 2801 John Street, Markham Ontario, Canada L3R 1B4
Penguin Books (NZ) Ltd, 182-190 Wairau Road, Auckland 10, New Zealand

Penguin Books Ltd, Registered Offices: Harmondsworth, Middlesex, England

First published 1990

Copyright © Jill and Martin Leman, 1990

Made and printed in
Great Britain by William Clowes Limited,
Beccles and London.

Typeset by Pastiche, London

A CIP catalogue record for this book is available from the British Library.

Library of Congress Catalog Card No: 90-60961

ISBN 07207 1971 2